QUIET LABOR

To Pandelis & Julia,

"The margins are weeping & fill with rumors"

with love & appreciation,

ELIOT CARDINAUX

Eliot Cardinaux

THE BODILY PRESS
Amherst, MA

All poetry by Eliot Cardinaux except where indicated.
First Edition. Copyright © 2024 Eliot Cardinaux

This book is set in Garamond Premier Pro and Optima.
Book design and layout by Eliot Cardinaux.
eliotcardinaux.com

Cover artwork by Peter Knapp
All Rights Reserved Copyright © 2022 Peter Knapp
Detail from "Wonder's Wanderings."
Mixed media. 31" h x 27⅜" w
PeterKnappArt.com

Bodily Press logo designed by Katya Popova.
popova.space

QUIET LABOR

*in memory of Daniel Levine,
trumpeter, composer, friend.*
3/18/1985 — 2/7/2022

Table of Contents

Horseshoes & Rings / ix

◆

THE LEGATO BRAID

A Bridge of Flowers / 17
Rumors / 18
Said Regression / 20
Beginners Meeting / 22
Haiku / 23
You Rose / 24
Box / 26
Memory, Sadness Said / 28
Trivial Adornments / 32
Horizon / 33
Jerusalem / 34
You Cathedral / 35
Post / 36
Mirrors / 38
Simile for War / 42
To Begin With / 43

◆

PART WAYS

Mirror Negative / 47
The Field / 49
Safe Passage / 51
Part Ways / 52
Freedom / 53
Narratives of the Strata / 54
Sleep Song / 66
Pietà / 68
Insomatic / 69
Extant Elegy / 70
Horseshoes / 71

◆

Acknowledgments / 73

Notes / 75

About the Author / 77

Horseshoes & Rings

This book chronicles a double loss. In the midst of my grief at the death of a friend and close musical ally, Daniel Levine, who died of an overdose in February 2022, I ended a long-term relationship with my partner of seven years who had been struggling with severe depression on and off (brought on, as we both learned, only later, by autoimmune disease), and who had been hospitalized on numerous occasions throughout our relationship. My ex-partner and I had only recently gotten sober from alcohol and other substances when Daniel opened up to me about his struggles with addiction. He and I talked at length about sobriety for a year before he died. He had enormous insight, but refused the twelve-step program which might have saved his life. My ex-partner was hospitalized again, for depression, the day after his funeral, which caused too great a rift in our romantic relationship for me to sustain my part in it.

Braiding these compounded losses together resulted in the poems in the first section of this book. Many of those poems take place, and were written, in liminal spaces — hospitals, AA meetings, funerals, Dunkin' Donuts, park benches, and the gallery where I often practiced piano at the time — spaces rife with the troubling safety of isolation, despite being surrounded by other people.

The poems in the second section of this book resulted from an effort to unbraid the two losses. Those poems are infused with a renewed perception of the world, common in grief, and the accompanying rush of memory, both personal and political. Daniel was Jewish, and queer, an activist who refused his birthright trip to Israel, and was involved in Occupy Wall Street at Zuccotti Park, where it began. He later came to interview Noam Chomsky, about the anarchist underpinnings of the movement, on New York City public radio. Daniel also witnessed 9/11 first-hand, from the windows of Stuyvesant High School. It affected him deeply.

The form of this book is a horseshoe, a broken ring, in the sense that the Russian-Jewish poet Osip Mandelstam wrote about, and could hardly achieve, because he lived his poetic life in secret. Not only hiding his manuscripts from the authorities, even the real-life references in Mandelstam's poems remain obscure, masked by images and associations, until his "Stalin Epigram" finally fated him to exile and eventual death, for speaking his mind directly. He writes — in translation here, by Clarence Brown and W. S. Merwin — in poem #123, in 1920, 18 years before his death:

> As it is we never emerge from the dance,
> from the ring, from the enchantment.

Daniel often told me not to hide behind my imagery. Though my poetry itself remains elliptical, I have no excuse but to address things here directly, if there is anything to be gained for a reader.

The "horseshoe" form of this book also hearkens back to John Coltrane, who talked about starting a musical sentence in the middle, and working outward, in "both directions at once." Mandelstam's poetry gave me the title of this collection (see my notes on page 75), and two lines by Paul Celan, from a book he dedicated to Mandelstam's memory, grace the first section as an epigraph. Coltrane's music, and his own journey through addiction and recovery, were a serious inspiration to Daniel, especially toward the end. It seems fitting that their spirits grace the work in unexpected ways.

Grief is never finished. It is a quiet labor, and ongoing. In trying to finish this collection, I wandered into an endgame I had to accept I could never win. This admission comes with the acknowledgment that my own grieving voice is one of many. The closing poem relays a dream I had, of the three of us —Daniel, my ex-partner, and me — shipwrecked in an overgrown junkyard, three abandoned pianos encircling us in a clearing. The only thing we could do in the dream was play, despite the finality of loss, the sadness of separation.

That music is central to this book is no accident. Daniel was an erudite composer, trumpet player, bandleader, poet, and avid reader — a potent influence on my development as an artist and human being. If you, reader, feel the desire to check his music out, search for his album *Knuckleball* on Bandcamp. He is sorely missed.

Eliot Cardinaux
March 18th, 2024

*the need gotta be
so deep words can't
answer simple questions*

—Yusef Komunyakaa, "Blue Light Lounge Sutra
For The Performance Poets At Harold Park Hotel"

THE LEGATO BRAID

O einer, o keiner, o niemand, o du:
Where did it lead, as it led nowhere?

—Paul Celan, *Die Niemandsrose*

A Bridge of Flowers

After

(it begins)

When wrath falls
& dusk wraps its curtain
around my love

(I am also
speechless)

Push through the screen
so the real is born
again

(a bridge of flowers
to our eyes)

In this world right now
if your hands can maintain it

(illuminating outlines
of a softer place)

Nothing will be
as it should be

(better than all we
began to hope for
as it falls away)

Rumors

I.
Death magnifies
her rattling hair
through the bleating
doors
exhausted
swinging tremors of sleep

II.
The rhyme divulges
a red thread
eyes red with impatience
envy it
the two gossip freely
as if in a stream

III.
Worlds
I could not remember
annulled by prayer
touch my ribs
& no one sees
what floods me

IV.
I bathe my head
in the dull yellow light
my love like this place
is liminal
the conduit of a newly
transparent voice

V.
Do we live
into little annihilations
if only you could hear
these knives of air
crushing hard song
into sugar

Said Regression

I get up in our story
& walk to the door

I think into the crowd
& with any slight envy
wear my crown

But the lead of language
sinks

They cried into onions

Fools like me in the rain

Like steel down a
garbage chute

Shrill in these times
of coal

Their tears

The intrusion of poetry
light bent out of shape
& eventually shattered

The mirror

Coins flattened
by trains

Loyalty never
lost to loved
ones

Beginners Meeting

She is not my beloved on Earth
who makes stone blush

That the hours come clumsy to handle
impractical hearts
& we stave them
off

If I lift this dull
& invincible hatch to fill the ventricle

Will they hang each cross to suffer
its torturous purpose
when music is not allowed
will the devil flinch

Haiku

I.
Shadowed poppy field
violent gust fleeting petals
thieved brainstems of youth

II.
Birch catkins dangle
toward a ravine in summer's
ransacked prose poem

You Rose

I.
Out of fog I heard you,
said your name

& stumbled like a bear
blind with bees

The air was thin
as if it pierced
an exquisite
honeycomb

From no one's home
I wandered
into this clay

Lungs filled I fled
till the wineskin broke &
venom bled out over
spring

II.
& I gently, gently laid
the bees in your hand

You swam in the silent
notch of the almond,
air wrung from heavy
wreaths

Till the crystal freezes,
until duress draws
a narrow path

See it now
in the doubled
grey twining of sky
& branches

Nothing
left inside emptiness
stutters your name

Box

I.
Each song is a sacrifice

No human
hand drops the needle now

Black strips of envy unfurling in Escher
mirrors

Maples breathe friendship around
the dead now no flutes in the manicured
canopy

Nothing allowed
to die here the dark ushers in
resistance

II.
It's been two days

I hope you're enjoying the sound
from Pandora's turntable

Torn off loop
of a mind if you have one

Little praise machine

Memory, Sadness Said

You cave-mouthed
crumbling distance

Swallowed these
shadows

Audiating dust
singing
holy mercury

Who cast up
signs

Behind these
walls
in the muses'
chatter

Beyond
space
& this
gapingness

Whose
maw said
mew

I ask

Who is lost in this body
repeat the spell

Throw more change
into the wick

Deposit your
departure
here

Drawn up
from a swell

I say
there's room for you

There's energy

Because of you
there's magic
in this tone

Vibration
in these long shadows

Tuned to so many
an analog flame

A shadow's
turbine

Grips
the light

The extended
nerve

Signals
the wave-
end

Havens

The shrieking
bulb

Deletes you

Crawling
on hands
of thought

Through
the shining
furrow

Storm this
thriving

Deepness
from
the weakness-
well

Our breath
within it

Sovereign under all
this meekness

Trivial Adornments

Nameless, your tears
still wet the laughing
Lenten rose

They have stolen
your evil
courage

The blush of
which lays new upon
each grief

Stagger in at the elbow
my fellow
        petal

We are left here
scattered

Liminal & bruising

Self-provoking such
a palpitation

Engines of
a giftless
verb

Horizon

The earth is a whetstone
singing
          incomparable words

Lay dark & beating,
heart
in the grave the sky made
                of apples

& the eyes of other
animals
redden in translation

Things that are leaving
after being said
begin to advertise the evening

Under the lindens
day will freeze up toward

Where if not far away

Jerusalem

To whom hope is a loss
of balance

Home vanished
& God
is a three-legged
ragdoll running

Hyenas the night only heard

To audiate these wars
three sets
of jaws & the blood the eyes
unknotted

Do not swim here

In slow roses
an origin grows
out of slim words
shocked clouds choked out
in fits of weeping

You Cathedral

Sudden
dark drew you in

Broken beams
lay dull weight
on your awkward
frame

The weathers of all
these years have emptied you

In the hollow
the notches lengthen
& violets
spring up in the silence

I turn to you slowly

With each stroke ink
sobs with the current

I drink this air
where the earth sings
rough edges of language
to quiet labor

Post

In my heart
sinks a coin
derived from
this

Two faces
in the cold
tearing myth
from myth

Adopt me

Rock me in witness
onto a leaf outside

I light a candle in my mouth
let the oar make
eddies around the word

I will not die of
its inaction,
troubled
blessing,
cave inside
the sign

A doorway not
yet inconsolable
I stand in

To enter the room
unfixed & dancing
splay my song
at you
homing
to your absence
like a migrant bird

Mirrors

I.
No one
has ever sculpted you

Memory bends
the light around us
as we live

Like whose wound &
whose hand runs along it
nulled by a thread

Torn
into shapes like this

What to make of the lull

Stitching
grace with
envy for us to hold

Lost like the rest

II.
What
red glare portending
nothing rolls there

Marbles in
a child's
eye

Flashes
back at what he saw

& lies between
the thing & the bending
out of it

A serpentine
shudder shutters out
this image
trying for what
he is

III.
It says something about us all

To be ordered
& plotted
further in

To let
someone suffer to
you

& pretend

Lost
gods are like
this

IV.
Would the rain fall through the grate

Would the peacefulness of it
spare us

Suffer what
no one
chose

Simile for War

To pull the thread of silence
rifle through eddies
echo to echo

For beauty a sinkhole
of cool green leafage
to course over stone

For threnodies of doves
to circle the ruin
of stolen country

In the lap of the water
dapples & horses
lulled by the world

To Begin With

Things are hushed now

Spring enrages you

We walk in the acoustics
between us

Each artifact an artifice
but lived

Sworn off these pages
in clear blue air

Who lingers with a touch of flame
on your eyelash

The margins are weeping
and fill with rumors

Spring enlarges us

We float with the pollen
clouding the data
that called us up

PART WAYS

And the sun still as strong as before.
Its impatient brushes were painting the world.

—Tomas Tranströmer, *Secrets on the Way*

Mirror Negative

Life bleeds through the map
of the zone we're in

In the old house coming

Wish for a room

Sound in a haze
clung to the dance there

In our buzzing
open throats

The thought accumulates

That the whole town is in mourning

Plays still on the morning air

Time & time again

It's wisdom confessing joy
under duress

Distressing the line
& laughing with it
before it can turn its head

Don't lean, my prophecy,
against the window

Something might
come tumbling through

The rain
trying to meet the dust,
the inside of grief

Your glinty eyes
telling me
I'm happy sad happy to see you

The Field

*to the death in blue night
of that faintly shining mind*

—Gennady Aygi

The mountain
landscape on our wall

The dangling
philodendron
& the toy
accordion

Next to the
thatched cat
in a chair made of
unstripped
twigs

& those two faces
carried me through freedom
onto the stubborn
grey field
of happiness

Where I am tormented
I am let go

That she set sail in the air
above the Ohio
the day I was born

& I was born aloft
on volcanic dust
over darkened Europe

My swallow the daughter of time
darts out of this honey
in twisted
shadows of the dead

To where night opens onto blue fields
& you gently recover from this

Safe Passage

It's a question of ruin,
things being unsaid by the wind

No two sides of departure,
delineation

Ten seconds before the last

& between each song
a skylark

A question of ash
& art

A fire
toward something else

What other than this

Part Ways

For a moment the sky is beneath me

Beautiful in that it can't be

Any other than abyss the unfeeling hurtle

Of sound in the engine of grief encased

In a box of shadow somehow providing

Enough static to power its churning

Thoughtpractice living from day to day

Inside of you look how it breathes out

The deep earth reversing gravity

Freedom

Something stranger than summer rain
cascades off the rooftop

Goldfinches
out of the nest
for the first time
gather in a moment
of solace

No, in sunshine

In your absence
you need this most

A low plane or a dragonfly
buzzes overhead

Whose eyes are blue enough to tell

Narratives of the Strata

I.
Look out at the absence

Eyes swimming
the mill of the sun

Whose double clock face
warps & whispers

Time is empty

Of every ascetic victory

Stand out in the world

Light darts like seed
from an invasive hand

A starling stands out
from its deeper shadow

Dislodging from strata
fossilized words

II.
The cat's shadow has left my room

She hides behind skirts of absence

In silence greater than any

Life schism in monostich

May petals fallen

As if from memory

Invisible to the touch

Like threads

From the here to the after

Rest at your feet in a fearful blush

III.
Youth locked in place
by the death of a singer

Troubled by oak trees

Dogeared by slender hands

This poem could take on the shape
of a sign of comfort

Cradled by impossible love

These fault lines of life on earth
have drawn curtains around them

All that is left behind
by freedom flickers
like a morning star

IV.
The dawn fury of tenements
(can you call them trees)

A long row of them crowded
with waking birds

I too am stranded
in the way of their cries

Skirting the edges
of barred horizon

Their outline illuminates
the dull face of the early sun

A grim power
lifts light from its shell

Delight
(it's too clear for memory)

V.
The memory a drawer
in a dream

Its contents obscured by
mischief

Seeds of rosehip

A plot from its shadow
severed

Hurtful itch

We are brought before dawn
to the landscape of Tautavel

Man made his skull here
an elongated prototype

The air grows still
with the heat of sunrise

& the crackle of countless
snails

We are punished
but not for this

VI.
I sit in what stares at me,
lonely

Glimpsed from an elevation

To write outside ethics
a listless brooding

Early script

Trees barely heaving,
digesting hoarsely

The course earth's
horror unhidden

Sublimating tracks in the dark

All powers eluding
conscious daylight

Impressed in silence

To dream you need
palm & pigment

VII.
Heat hangs like a brass plate
over the unintelligible
afternoon

In America whose flag
whispers sky through
traffic

Whose clouds roll reflected
in plexiglass

Where triumphant
corners reel

We fall for descriptions like these

But the mendicant
needs no features

He asks for cigarettes
that passersby can't likely
afford to give

VIII.
Something taken

A caravan crossing
the desert along
the horizon

A line of text

Slides off the force
of inaudible wailing

A drop of silver bromide
sweetens like this
into mother's milk

Misspellings
divert the river

Flowing from notebook to notebook
its letters scatter
like garden birds at the sight of a soldier
who sees the living scatter
in his dream of death

IX.
Entering my silent heaven
the radio crackles with forests

Daylight turns pages frantically

A car racing
toward summer's illusion, life gushes
from the plot of a mystery

A murderer twists
the knife in his victim's belly
& out of her mouth
spring forth the artificial
flowers of inheritance

A bookseller's sale cart
pushes itself in from the rain,
checks the weather,
& rolls out into the town square
now settled by grazing horses

A solution must turn the key,
like the answer to a novel chess move
in a position reached countless
times before

Into sunlight,
church bells chime
their revelation, last night's insects
scattered on the porch

X.
Solitude

A spider in moonlight
between two trees

& even then the need
for quiet labor

Ernesto wrangling the stones

& the fire a brooding
jealousy toward the entrancement

The light electric & the skin
salt-gleaming

The porous air felt simple
& we obeyed

Fine child's paintbrush
touch up the sky's blue-silver

Your voice of silver
somehow unbetrayed

XI.
Hot wind
coming up the Heights
I stand in it blazing at the gate

At the marrow of choice
& freedom bright fire in the
bones I climb to the third floor

Where you put on a record, seamlessly
weave into it & talk in simple terms

O my beloved
how sweet it is
to go down
and bathe in the pool
before your eyes
letting you see how
my drenched linen dress
marries
the beauty of my body
Come, look at me

XII.
For words I am too
overwhelmed not
to break your likeness

Shirt
the water married
to your body

No statue to live by
shadowlike to offend
& validate

Cool musics venting you
to want them shifting

The modern opening
of dawn to raise the stars

A memory of terror

Pavane not a dead pavane,
a sixth made to ring
with the number of living ends

Home changes
as you are released

Sleep Song

Along the morning's shoreline
new pathways emerge
from a sportscaster's voice

A rockbound pine
on a miniature island

My attention fumbles
with inaudible verbs,
like a tow-rope cast in
from the fog

My nightmares
struggle against
the silk of sleep

Where life's constellation
of unanswered questions
has tethered its inmost
injured melody

Roots below the earth seem
to sting her

The green sky rings with raindrops

Trees glisten wide & fade

Their absence stirs
the hammer of my ear
& it quakes like
poplar leaves

Words break free
at the point of waking

Pietà

Unfinished
the landlocked sadness

Two rowers meet with the fog

Before the sun has risen fully
taking up its crest

The energy wafts in waves
down my back

Pure stillness

How can the trees stand it

A tanker's foghorn
peels away the world
with the pain of tectonic plates

A movement among the shoulder blades
of a young man searching the same town
for detail
                he cannot find here

Something pushes me from far away

Insomatic

This is just endgame

A long slow rippling analysis
in candor
on the periphery

Till morning comes
in blush on the page

Where two bodies threaded
with birdsong are blown away

& the haze of their static ruptures
atomized appearance

Light incubates its travel in this way

It hides its face in shadow

The inverted projections
dance
on the back of the throat
like this like this

Extant Elegy

An unstable window roars

A river of light
in jagged edges: *I*

No single one but they come like
color in the wave of day

Vine or vane of what's poised
in weather, bruising their own
vernacular

So time creeps
with adjoining light,

With the sudden extent of their virtue,
forming a swarm

Of measure
plaguing the evident

The glossary of wounds
left blank

Horseshoes

Time hasn't caught up with me

Three pianos ring a clearing

We mess at horseshoes in the trash
targeting the joints of an unknown scale

Whole note, half-tone, linger-tone, third

We've given up on waking

You've walked right to the edge of the field

A murmuration hums in a grey mood
above the turbines

The thrall of stasis

You swerve at the vanishing point

Each patented signal wafts over
an outsized age

Acknowledgments

My sincere thanks to the editors of the following journals in which these poems first appeared:

"A Bridge of Flowers" in *Solstice*.

"Said Regression" in *The Arts Fuse*.

"Beginners Meeting" and "Trivial Adornments" in *Meat for Tea*.

An earlier version of "Memory, Sadness Said" in *Café Review*.

Sections I. & III. of "Narratives of the Strata" in *Spoon River Poetry Review*, as "Look out at the absence," and "Flight," alongside "Insomatic," "Extant Elegy," and "Horseshoes."

Versions of these poems also appeared in the following chapbooks from The Bodily Press: *The Margins Weep Slow Roses* (2022); *Narratives of the Strata* (2022); and *Caprice* (2023).

I am vastly grateful to Ivy Schweitzer for her friendship, editing skills, and unwavering support in helping me put this book together.

A heartfelt thank you to Sammy Lê, for sitting with these poems many an evening.

A very deep bow to Peter Gizzi and Ocean Vuong for their mentorship and guidance over the years.

Profound gratitude to Jade Welch (*née* Wollin) for sharing in this experience.

Love and thanks to Bram Kincheloe, Flin van Hemmen, Sean Ali, Ryan Snow, Steven Long, Will McEvoy, Adam Chilenski, Greg Paulus, Ryan Blotnick, Isaac Luxon, Nick Messitte, Devin Gray, and Ben Capps, for sharing in this love and grief.

Deep gratitude to drummer/percussionist Gary Fieldman for performing on the album *Pavane* (Bodily Press, 2022), a companion piece to this book, and to Warren Amerman who recorded, mixed, mastered, and co-produced the record.

A special thank you to Peter Knapp for the kind use of his beautiful artwork.

Finally, a heartfelt thank you to my parents, my two sisters, and all my extended family, for always being there.

Notes

The title of this book is borrowed from a poem by Osip Mandelstam. I give it back to him. The poem reads as follows, translated by Clarence Brown and W. S. Merwin, in *The Selected Poems of Osip Mandelstam* (NYRB, 2004):

> What has held out against oxidation
> and adulteration, burns like feminine silver,
> and quiet labor silvers the iron plow
> and the poet's voice.
>
> Voronezh [1937]

The epigraph at the beginning of this collection is taken from Yusef Komunyakaa's *Neon Vernacular: New and Selected Poems* (Wesleyan University Press, 1993).

The epigraph at the beginning of the first section of this book is taken from the opening poem in Paul Celan's *Die Niemandsrose* (*NoOnesRose*), as collected in *Memory Rose into Threshold Speech: The Collected Earlier Poetry*, Pierre Joris, translator (FSG, 2020). The first line appears in the original German for the sake of its music.

The epigraph at the beginning of the second section of this book is taken from the title poem of Tomas Tranströmer's *Secrets on the Way*, collected in *The Great Enigma: New Collected Poems*, Robin Fulton, translator (New Directions, 2011).

The poem "Jerusalem" derives from *Concerto Al-Quds*, a book of poetry written by the Syrian poet Adonis on the city of Al-Quds (Jerusalem), Khaled Mattawa, translator (Yale University Press, 2017).

The poems "Mirrors" and "Mirror Negative" derive in part from imagery in Andrei Tarkovsky's films, *Stalker* (Mosfilm, 1979), and *Mirror* (Mosfilm, 1975).

The epigraph at the beginning of "The Field" is from Gennady Aygi's poem "Dream: Flight of the Dragonfly," as collected in *Into the Snow: Selected Poems of Gennady Aygi*, Sarah Valentine, translator (Wave Books, 2011).

In Section XI. of "Narratives of the Strata," the stanza in italics is taken verbatim from "Poem inscribed on an Egyptian statue, 1500 BC," as transcribed and included in John Berger's essay "The Hour of Poetry," collected in *The Sense of Sight* (Knopf Doubleday, 2011).

About the Author

ELIOT CARDINAUX is a poet, pianist, composer, and translator working at the edges of the lyric and improvised music. The author of *On the Long Blue Night* (Dos Madres, 2023), and the trio of *Quiet Labor*, *Toy Elegy*, and *This Music From Another Room* (Bodily Press, 2024), as well as numerous chapbooks, Cardinaux has also produced and appeared on over a dozen albums of original music, including *American Thicket* (Loyal Label, 2016); *Out of Our Systems* and *Pavane* (Bodily Press, 2022); and most recently *Imminence* (self-released, 2024) with American percussionist Gary Fieldman. He holds a bachelor's degree in contemporary improvisation from The New England Conservatory of Music, and an MFA in creative writing, with a focus on poetry, from the University of Massachusetts in Amherst. Eliot's poems and translations have appeared in journals such as *California Quarterly*, *Tupelo Quarterly*, *Meridian*, *Jacket2*, *The Arts Fuse*, *Bennington Review*, *Solstice*, and *Spoon River Poetry Review*. At present, he co-leads an American trio with bassist Will McEvoy and drummer Max Goldman, works in a duo with Gary Fieldman, leads his own Danish Quartet, and is a member of the European-based free-improvisation ensemble, Our Hearts as Thieves. He has appeared, in various settings, with musicians such as Kresten Osgood, Mat Maneri, Randy Peterson, Thomas Morgan, Asger Thomsen, Ryan Blotnick, Eivind Opsvik, Niels Vincentz, Taus Bregnhøj-Olesen, Isaac Luxon, Flin van Hemmen, and Mia Dyberg. He performs throughout Europe and the Northeast United States. He has taught literature and writing at UMass Amherst, and works as a bookseller at Amherst Books. He is the sole founder and editor of The Bodily Press.

Author photograph by poet Denver Butson • denverbutson.com

THE BODILY PRESS
bodilypress.bandcamp.com